IMAGES
of America

WYOMING

HERE AND ON THE COVER: Gypsum mines were big business in Wyoming, beginning in 1842, and were located along Plaster Creek. The mine shown on the cover was owned by Bert Kragt. His son Paul is operating the drill here. As people were gradually depleting the mines, the family turned theirs into the Michigan Cold Storage Company, now operated by grandson Ronald P. Kragt. (Grand Rapids Public Library.)

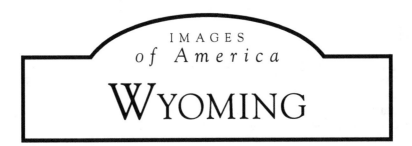

IMAGES
of America

WYOMING

Norma Lewis and Jay de Vries

ARCADIA
PUBLISHING

Published by Arcadia Publishing
Charleston, South Carolina

Library of Congress Control Number: 2010926578

For all general information, please contact Arcadia Publishing:
Telephone 843-853-2070
Fax 843-853-0044
E-mail sales@arcadiapublishing.com
For customer service and orders:
Toll-Free 1-888-313-2665

Visit us on the Internet at www.arcadiapublishing.com

For our families, with love and appreciation

CONTENTS

Acknowledgments   6

Foreword   7

Introduction   9

1.   The Early Years   11

2.   Commerce and Industry   29

3.   Schools   61

4.   Churches   79

5.   Everyday Life in Wyoming   87

6.   Looking Ahead   119

ACKNOWLEDGMENTS

Many, many thanks go to David Harris and Rhonda Ayers for stepping up and offering assistance. And to Ron Strauss, we appreciate you offering so many wonderful images and having the foresight to save them for posterity. We also thank Robert Kline for the images found on his Web site, a marvelous collection of Godwin Heights history.

A huge thank you goes to the Wyoming Historical Society, especially Bill Branz, for opening their collections to us. This book would not be as complete without this support.
Again, we want to thank the Grand Rapids Public Library for their ongoing assistance, especially Karolee Hazelwood, who always comes through with scans of our selections from the treasure trove of possibilities.

To the companies, schools, churches, and individuals whose materials appear within: thank you. Thank you for saving your histories, and thank you for sharing them.

We are indebted to everyone at Arcadia Publishing, from Anna Wilson and John Pearson in Chicago, to all of you in South Carolina who keep everything on track and running so smoothly.

As always, we thank our families for their continued interest in and enthusiasm for our projects. We love you all and rely on your support.

FOREWORD

"If you need water, annex or bring a teacup." These were the words purportedly stated by the political fathers in the city of Grand Rapids when Wyoming Township leaders came to purchase water in the mid-1950s. Water wars were not just a Wild West irony, it was happening in west Michigan as well. Thus, in 1959, the city of Wyoming was born, conceived in defiance to the big city next door. From day one, Wyoming residents were determined to decide their own future: a city of our vision and progress.

One of the first ventures was the building of a freshwater treatment plant on the shores of Lake Michigan, north of Holland. This availability of a major residential/commercial commodity gave opportunity for planned growth, and Wyoming grew as a blue-collar, workingman's community. It was a good place to find a job and a great place to raise a family. Homes, churches, schools, businesses, and factories all flourished.

The South Beltline (Twenty-eighth Street) became home to the first shopping mall, Rogers Plaza, and the Rogers Department Store, which started as a blue jeans and work-clothing retailer to become a state-wide phenomenon of quality shopping. Down the road a bit was Studio 28, home to more movie screens than any other location in Michigan.

Transportation access for businesses and families was very important. With Chicago Drive on the north and east, U.S. 131 running north and south on the east, and Forty-fourth Street (pre-M-6) on the south, growth meant opportunities. Division Avenue from Twenty-eighth Street to Thirty-second Street became used-car alley, and retail of every variety sprung up in Godwin Heights at Thirty-sixth Street to Home Acres at Forty-fourth Street.

Politically Wyoming could be defiant, even among its own. A majority of the city council members were once recalled, and the governor had to appoint people to run the city. Wyoming became the second largest city in west Michigan. To some of its neighboring cities, Wyoming was the "big-sister sibling," not needing services from Grand Rapids like the others. It became freshwater and wastewater treatment providers for many of west Michigan's communities.

In 1938, in the second house west of the Fisher Body Plant on Allen Road (now Thirty-sixth Street and Clay), Harold was born the youngest of five in a Dutch family. In 1948, his father began a food-distribution business on Olympia Street between Division and Burlingame Avenues. We sold local bakery products, like Delight Donuts, Dixie Cream donuts, Tip-Top Cakes, and Mrs. Wagner's Pies. The company was registered as Serve-U-Cake Distributing; service was its forte.

Public service became our calling when, in 1987, Harold was elected city council member at-large. From 1989 to 1992, he served as mayor. In 1993, he became the state representative for the district that includes Wyoming, serving six years until term limits restricted him from running again. Then Joanne was elected and also served six years as state representative. Since 2002, Harold has been a Kent County commissioner, again serving the people of Wyoming. In 2007, Joanne was elected Third Ward councilwoman in Wyoming and continues serving. Both enjoy elected public service.

What is Wyoming's future? Some manufacturing plants have been reduced or eliminated. The job market is tough, but the people of Wyoming are tough as well. The demographics are changing, yet opportunities are here. Nothing happens until something is sold; Wyoming must keep selling itself and find products and services to sell to others, bringing continued prosperity for its wonderful residents.

—Harold J. and Joanne M. Voorhees

INTRODUCTION

Wyoming, located in Kent County, was first settled in 1832 and prospered because Buck Creek provided power and transportation. In 1848, the early settlement split, and the southern portion became Byron Center while the northern part became Wyoming Township. It wasn't until 1959, the same year Alaska and Hawaii became states, that the city incorporated to protect itself from the threats of further annexation from both Grand Rapids and Grandville.

Dr. Electus B. Ward settled in northeast Wyoming in 1881 and built a 280-acre estate that he called Clyde Park in honor of his prized Clydesdale horses. The original house was destroyed by fire in 1916, but the name lives on as the property's boundary touched on what is now Clyde Park Avenue on one of the city's main north-south streets.

General Motors opened its first Wyoming facility in 1936, attracting workers—many of who became residents. During the post–World War II years, Wyoming experienced phenomenal growth. Industry in the area led to residential growth as well. People had the enviable lifestyle of short commutes to good-paying jobs, a good school system for their children, churches, parks, and shopping—all without leaving Wyoming.

Merchants in the city weren't just there to make a quick buck. They were an integral part of the larger community. Earl Robson (of the Robson Department Store) hosted an annual anniversary sale, where he served cake and coffee to the local dignitaries as well as hundreds of customers. The cakes grew larger as years went by, with the 45th anniversary cake in 1972 weighing in at 500 pounds. The store remained in business until 1976, a total of 48 years. In addition to his store, Robson served Wyoming as a city council member for more than nine years.

Marge Wilson, owner of Marge's Donut Den, exemplifies the kind of community-minded business owner who keeps smaller cities afloat. She opens her shop on Christmas Day because some of her customers have nowhere else to go. She allows a Bible study group to meet in her shop, and she even hosted a small wedding when the bride and groom were short on funds and wanted something more meaningful than a city hall ceremony.

When Hyman Berkowitz (known popularly as Mr. Berk) opened what became the upscale Rogers Department Store, customers descended upon Wyoming from all over the Grand Rapids area. Though Jewish, he demonstrated his sensitivity to the beliefs of his clientele by offering clergy discounts and never opening on Sundays, even after the malls began doing so. After he closed the store in 2003, the city held a ceremony in recognition of Mr. Berk and his wife, Gretta, for their longtime contributions to Wyoming.

Wyoming fell into a decline in recent years. Many of the more affluent residents moved to nearby suburbs like Jenison and Hudonsville, but the community has reemerged. There is now a large Latin American population in the city (close to 15 percent), as well as Asian and African American. The newcomers have become homeowners who take pride in maintaining their dwellings. New companies are moving in to replace those that have closed or moved on, and there is a spirit of optimism as the city looks ahead.

One

THE EARLY YEARS

In its earliest days, Wyoming was populated by the prehistoric Hopewell Indians. Their burial mounds still can be found in the region, though most have been leveled. Unlike some regions, when the white settlers came the Indians welcomed and helped them.

Most of the pioneers were farmers, and they attracted the blacksmiths, merchants, teachers, ministers, and others who responded to their needs. Industry followed, and the township soon became the largest in the region outside of Grand Rapids; it remains so today. Some of the early settlers started companies that remain in business and are still owned by the founding families. The Koeze Company is one. Michigan Natural Storage is another, with Ronald Kragt operating a cold-storage facility in the old gypsum mine his grandfather and father operated before him.

Once the second busiest road in the state, Twenty-eighth Street started out as a dirt road called Beals. One of the main north-south roads, Division Avenue, began as a plank road named Gull Prairie Road.

The growing population needed schools. The first in the Godwin area opened in 1843, with other Wyoming district schools following in the 1850s—a couple of decades before school attendance became mandatory. Wyoming's first church, Grandville Avenue Christian Reformed, opened in 1891 and is still going strong, though a merger changed its name to the Roosevelt Park Community Christian Reformed Church. Prior to its formation, township residents traveled to Grand Rapids, Byron Center, or Paris Township to attend services.

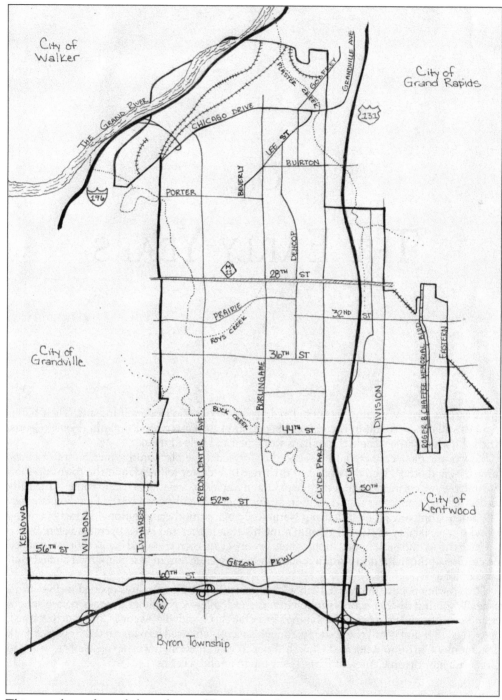

This map shows the early boundaries of Byron Township and the cities of Grand Rapids, Walker, Grandville, and Kentwood. (Jillian Berry.)

Long before white settlers discovered the Grand River valley, the Hopewell Indians populated the area. Some of their burial mounds are still in place and can be seen along Indian Mounds Drive. In 1966, the burial mounds were put on the National Register of Historic Places. (Grand Rapids Public Library.)

NORTON MOUND GROUP

HAS BEEN DESIGNATED A
REGISTERED NATIONAL
HISTORIC LANDMARK

UNDER THE PROVISIONS OF THE
HISTORIC SITES ACT OF AUGUST 21, 1935
THIS SITE POSSESSES EXCEPTIONAL VALUE
IN COMMEMORATING OR ILLUSTRATING
THE HISTORY OF THE UNITED STATES

U.S. DEPARTMENT OF THE INTERIOR
NATIONAL PARK SERVICE

1966

This 1900 photograph depicts some of the men who dredged the Grand River. Those identified include John Verstrate (fourth from left), Gus Closterhouse (seventh from left), Cass De Puit (third from right), and Charles Moody (far right). Mrs. John Porter is shown wearing a long apron and standing by her husband; their daughter is wearing a black skirt. (Wyoming Historical Commission.)

One of the earliest settlers, Jonathan F. Chubb, came to the area in 1825 for the purpose of operating a blacksmith shop at the Thomas Mission started in 1823 by Rev. Isaac McCoy. Other mission workers, including three other blacksmiths and a schoolteacher, came about the same time. This was 23 years before Wyoming Township organized and broke away from Byron Township. (Grand Rapids Public Library.)

Typical of the Wyoming farms before the start of the 20th century is this one operated by the Peterson family on what is now Kenowa Avenue. Even the cat came out to say "cheese." (Ron Strauss.)

When farm families took pictures, it wasn't unusual to include livestock and pets. This couple proudly shows their horse, while the chickens also get in on the act. (Wyoming Historical Commission.)

Jared Keyes was a truck farmer and grew his produce at 112 Allen Road, now Thirty-sixth Street. In the late 1950s, the farmhouse was razed, and an office building occupies the now commercially zoned property. (Wyoming Historical Commission.)

The driver of this horse and buggy needed his lap robe while traveling through the snow-covered streets. Note the windmill in the background. (Wyoming Historical Commission.)

Dutch immigrant Hendrik Geukes, at left, sits in a chair made in one of the Grand Rapids furniture factories where he found work when he first arrived from the old country. His two sons and two daughters are pictured below, all of who lived on Godfrey Avenue. They are (first row) Johanna Mengerink and John Geukes; (second row) Bernadine Siebers and Ben Geukes. (Ron Strauss.)

It is unknown if this event is a tea party or perhaps a Bible study group. The tablecloth and fine china indicate it is a special occasion rather than a routine break in the activities of a busy day. (Wyoming Historical Commission.)

John Westra poses with daughters Elizabeth and Mary and sons John Jr. (standing) and Jacob. His wife, Minnie, died of pneumonia in 1896. Shortly after this c. 1900 photograph was taken, Westra married Edith Boone of Illinois, and the family relocated to Chicago. (Westra family.)

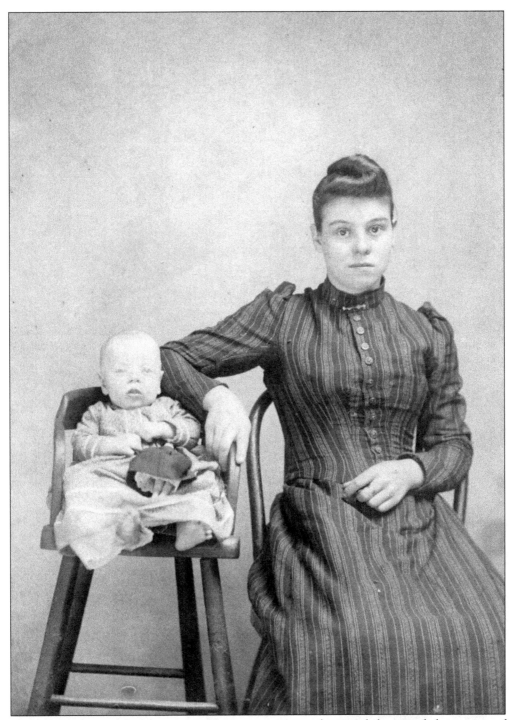

High chairs were wonderful inventions for youngsters at mealtime and also provided escape-proof seating for taking pictures. This is believed to be Delbert, the youngest of Lyman and Della (pictured) Conner's children. (Wyoming Historical Commission.)

Wyoming's brutal winters were no match for this ornate heater. The Visser babies slept soundly and snugly next to it. (Wyoming Historical Commission.)

These employees of the Alabastine plant pose in front of the gypsum mine located west of Plaster Creek on Chicago Drive. William Schultz is leaning against the loading dock ledge to the far left. Frank "Spike" Schultz is fourth from left in the second row. He became a boxer and was killed in a barroom brawl in Texas where he was chasing Pancho Villa. (Michigan Natural Storage.)

N. E. Smith and his wife are pictured here standing in front of the retail store he operated on Lee Street in Wyoming Park. (Wyoming Historical Commission.)

H. Husselman operated his harness and dry goods store on Burton Street until 1915, when he joined his brother Thomas to start a home construction business in the growing Home Acres area. (Wyoming Historical Commission.)

Almara and Minnie Kice owned this house on McKee Avenue, one of the first in the neighborhood, when McKee was still a dirt road. (Wyoming Historical Commission.)

Retail stores were the heart of the community. The Watson Brothers ran this store until 1918, after which the Gezon family bought and operated it. (Ron Strauss.)

The Geukes Meat Market (formerly called the Galewood Market) was located in this building at 1000 Burton Avenue before moving to Byron Center because the structure was destroyed by fire. (Ron Strauss.)

This 1918 Ford Model T truck is identical to the one driven by the Koeze family for making deliveries in the early days of the business. Today the company specializes in peanut butter and candy products. Current owner Jeff Koeze found this truck and had it restored to display in the Burlingame Avenue retail shop. (Jeff Koeze.)

Music played an important part in the education of children and in family entertainment. This girl takes a break from her piano practice to relax and hold her doll. (Wyoming Historical Commission.)

A branch of the prominent Wyoming Visser family poses outside their early-1900s farmhouse. (Wyoming Historical Commission.)

This charming booklet was given to students at the Emmons Fractional No. 3 School at the end of the 1908 school year. Students included eight first graders, two second graders, six third graders, no fourth-grade students, two fifth graders, four sixth graders, five seventh graders, and one each in eighth and ninth grades. School board members were Harry Emmons, Charles Ferrand, and Edward Troost. (Wyoming Historical Commission.)

The forerunner of Division Avenue was the Gull Prairie Plank Road connecting Grand Rapids and Kalamazoo. These horse-and-buggy travelers bump along the road south of Wyoming in the late 1860s. (Robert Kline.)

Two

COMMERCE AND INDUSTRY

The city thrived over the years, attracting heavy industry. General Motors opened a second plant on Burlingame Avenue. World War II brought Reynolds Metals Company. When Kentucky-based founder Richard Reynolds Sr. believed the war would be fought in the air, he opened three manufacturing facilities to provide lightweight aluminum extruded parts for the war effort. He chose Wyoming as one of his sites. First called Extruded Metals, it became a major employer and supplier of many industries, including aluminum automobile bumpers during the 1970s and early 1980s. The plant closed in 1990 after becoming antiquated and deemed too costly to renovate.

Leonard Refrigeration, which became Kelvinator and then Nash Kelvinator, was a major employer. So too were Lear Siegler and Bell Fibre. The one promising start-up that never got off the ground was picric acid plant, which was in the construction stage during World War I. The facility was expected to produce the acid used in poisonous mustard gas and would eventually employ 2,000 workers. The war ended in 1918, when only the two chimneys had been constructed. The project was never completed, and the chimneys were finally leveled in 1977. The Leonard E. Kaufman Golf Course now occupies the site. Gordon Food Service and Koeze's are headquartered here. Other employers include Benetler Automotive, Michigan Turkey Producers, Country Fresh Dairy, Pratt Industries (the former Bell Fibre), and Gainey Transportation.

Earl Robson's Department Store had long been a Division Avenue fixture when a point came where it was possible to avoid shopping in Grand Rapids completely. Southwest Michigan's first enclosed shopping mall, Rogers Plaza, opened in 1961 on the south side of Twenty-eighth Street, with Montgomery Ward and Kroger as anchors. A new shopping center, Southland, soon sprouted across Michael Avenue and boasted a Wurzburg store that later became Herpolshimers. Several grocers and early supermarkets kept residents' pantries well stocked. Among them were Meijer, Haan's, Steve DeYoung's Big Top, and Fred's Trading Post.

Tommy Brann's (home of the southwest Michigan favorite tri-tip sizzler) offered dining, as did Mr. Steak, Beltline Bar, Log Cabin Bar-B-Q, and the Swiss Chalet among others. More casual food could also be found. Everyone remembers Kum Bak burgers.

Gypsum mining was big business, and the mine owners sometimes offered tours or even held social events underground. These visitors line up at the well-laid buffet table. (Michigan Natural Storage.)

This photograph was a 1929 advertisement for the Majestic Radio Company. The men took the radio into the mine and were amazed when they received a signal from as far away as Texas. Because the mines were under both Wyoming and Grand Rapids, the exact location of this mine is undetermined, but it is believed to be in Wyoming. (Grand Rapids Public Library.)

Since 1957, the former gypsum mine, now called Michigan Natural Storage, has been used for cold storage. School groups have long been given tours to learn about the early mining days in the Wyoming–Grand Rapids area and about plaster. Burger Chef, whose cartons are shown, was a longtime fixture on Twenty-eighth Street. (Michigan Natural Storage.)

The picric acid plant smokestacks loomed over the Wyoming landscape for decades before being dismantled in 1977. Construction began during World War I, but when the war ended the project was abandoned. Homes were constructed on part of the property, and the Leonard E. Kaufman Golf Course is also on the site. (Wyoming Historic Commission.)

When General Motors's Fisher Body Division decided to build a stamping plant at Thirty-sixth Street and Buchanan Avenue in 1936, it brought new life into post-Depression Wyoming with its promise of growth and jobs. Here construction has begun. (Wyoming Historical Commission.)

Office furniture giant Steelcase began operations in 1912 as Metal Office Furniture at the Division Avenue facility shown above. As the company expanded over the years, it outgrew the original space and relocated a few miles east on Eastern Avenue, where Wyoming, Kentwood, and Grand Rapids meet. In the multibuilding complex below, only the building to the far right is in Wyoming. (Steelcase.)

Employees and guests tour the General Motors stamping facility on Thirty-sixth Street after one of its many expansions over the years. The plant was phased out in 2010 but will be remembered as one of the region's major employers. (Wyoming Historical Commission.)

In 1954, Local 730 (United Auto Workers) of the Wyoming General Motors stamping plant sent Paul Blake (holding pen in right hand), Ray Trent (behind UAW sign), and Art Heimer (with ribbon on the jacket) as delegates to the CIO (Congress of Industrial Organizations) convention. (Press Picture Service.)

In 1965, fellow workers gathered around Lee Vitch (in white shirt and tie) to celebrate his retirement. Hopefully he made good use of those golf clubs. (Local 730, United Auto Workers.)

The Nash Kelvinator Corporation, then named the Leonard Refrigeration Company, moved from Grand Rapids to Wyoming in 1910 and produced wooden iceboxes long before making the sleek refrigerators seen in this 1950 photograph. (Grand Rapids Public Library.)

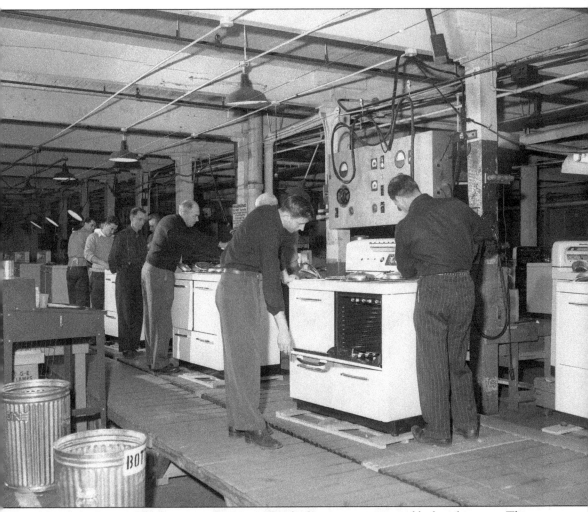

Also at the Leonard Refrigeration Company, finished stoves are inspected before shipment. This photograph was taken in January 1950. (Grand Rapids Public Library.)

George Clark, president of the Wyoming Chamber of Commerce, was on hand with his shovel in 1942 when the Extruded Metals Company broke ground for a plant to produce aluminum extrusions during the World War II effort. The post-war extrusions were used in a variety of industries, and the company changed its name to Reynolds Metals. (Grand Rapids Public Library.)

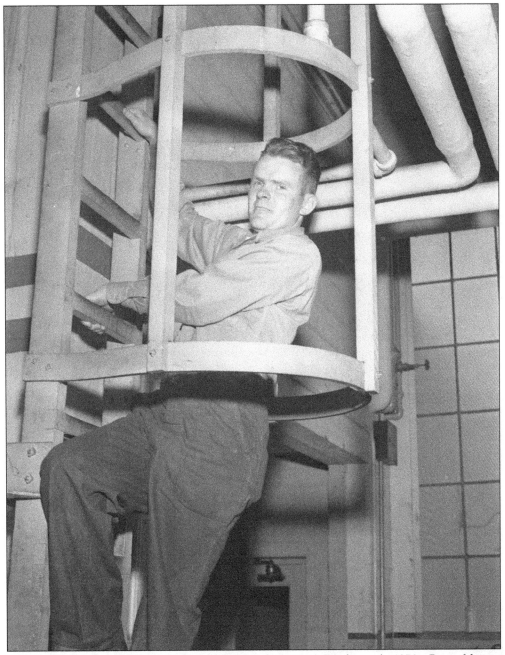

A Reynolds crane operator poses here on the job in 1946. By the early 1970s, Reynolds was producing bumpers for Ford Motor Company's Fairmont and Zephyr models, as well as for General Motors' Camaros and Vegas. (Grand Rapids Public Library.)

Local industry rallied to support the World War II effort, both during and after the war. The General Motors stamping plant turns out antiaircraft weapons at Thirty-sixth Street in this photograph. (Wyoming Historical Commission.)

Manufacturing companies did their part by employing permanently injured veterans and retraining them to make a living despite their disabilities. A veteran blinded in action works at his job at Kelvinator. (Grand Rapids Public Library.)

Everyone enjoyed the General
Motors diesel equipment plant's 1947
Christmas party. Just ask the boy
with the popgun. Santa also came
to the party, much to the delight
of the children in the image below.
(Grand Rapids Public Library.)

Women went to work in the factories during the World War II years and proved their ability to do the job. Many stayed on, like these ladies shown at the diesel equipment plant on Burlingame Avenue in 1950. (Grand Rapids Public Library.)

Ernie, the Keebler Company elf, stands guard outside the bakery at 310 Twenty-eighth Street. The Hekman Biscuit Company was taken over by Keebler in the 1960s. Today it has changed names once again and is now owned by the Kellogg Company of Battle Creek, Michigan. The factory is in a portion of Wyoming that was annexed by Grand Rapids and was one the reasons Wyoming incorporated as a city in 1959—to protect itself from future annexation attempts. (Grand Rapids Public Library.)

This aerial view shows the Lear Siegler Company, which was located in the Roger B. Chaffee Industrial Park area. Lear became Smiths Industries and is now owned by General Electric. (Grand Rapids Public Library.)

Gordon Food Service, now headquartered in Wyoming, started in Grand Rapids in 1897. By 1962, the company had relocated to the Clay Avenue building shown below, where they experienced phenomenal growth both in the United States and Canada. In addition to supplying the food-service industry, there are now retail outlets open to the public. Shown above is the third generation of corporate leadership. Pictured from left to right are John (president), Ben, Frank, and Paul Gordon. (Gordon Food Service.)

Waalkes Bakery, shown here around 1910, was a fixture on Chicago Drive and eventually evolved into a grocery store. It remains in business at the original location. (Ron Strauss.)

Wyoming was an industrial town, but small businesses also played an important part in its growth. The Visser Plumbing Company was a good example of an owner mixing business with community pride. This photograph is actually an advertisement that appeared in the 1928 Lee High School yearbook. (Wyoming Historic Commission.)

Darwin Peavey stands in front of the 1930s-style gas pumps at the Pennsylvania gas station. The glass containers allowed customers to see the amount of gas they were receiving, assuring them they weren't being cheated. This was in the days when gas sold for 14¢ a gallon, and this station had a different brand and grade in each pump. (Robert Kline.)

The Root Beer Wagon was a popular curb service stop during the 1940s and early 1950s. Located at 2907 Division Avenue, it closed in 1953 to make way for a used-car lot. (Robert Kline.)

The new Nash models are proudly being shown off here at Clock Motor Sales in the days before American-made cars were limited to the "Big Three": Ford, General Motors, and Chrysler. (Grand Rapids Public Library.)

This Packard is getting the full treatment from Smith's Auto Service in 1930. The shop was located on Division Avenue just south of Thirty-second Street. (Robert Kline.)

It always pays for a businessperson to keep his or her name in front of customers as Bob Christian Sr. did by sending holiday cards for the Division Avenue Bus Line, Inc., of which he was president and general manager. (Robert Kline.)

MERRY CHRISTMAS

and a very
Happy New Year

Robert Christian, Sr.
President & General Mgr.

DIVISION AVENUE BUS LINE, Inc.
Serving South Kent for 34 years.

THE H. D. LEE CO., INC.
DISTRIBUTION CENTER

From his earliest days in retail, Robson sold denim work clothing and bought large quantities from the H. D. Lee Company. When he took up long-distance walking as a health regimen, it was only fitting that he stroll down to Nashville, Tennessee, to call on his longtime supplier. (Wyoming Historical Commission.)

During World War II, Earl Robson, owner of the Robson Department Store on Division Avenue, invited local families of servicemen and women to post their loved one's photographs in his store windows. The number reached 2,200, and Robson kept the lights on at night to illuminate them for passersby to see. (Wyoming Historical Commission.)

Earl Robson poses with his family, employees, and friends in his Home Acres area department store on Division Avenue in the early 1940s. From left are Sandra Robson, Earl, Bonnie Robson, Bernice Pierce, Herb Myrick, Paul Greinke, Ann Robson, and Rita Oriole. (Wyoming Historical Commission.)

Ever the innovative merchandiser and publicist, Robson showed movies in his store basement during the Depression, initiated a Santa Claus parade, and held the area's first sidewalk sale. So it is no surprise that when he visited Norton, Virginia, and met the country music group the Bearded Beauties, he talked Wyoming officials into bringing them to the city to perform. They arrived in 1961—oxen, covered wagon, and all. (Wyoming Historical Commission.)

Clayton Brummel ran this 1957 advertisement in the October 24, 1957, edition of the *Photo Reporter*, describing a carload of Norge refrigerators priced at $149.95 and up with trade and "no reasonable offer refused." The company soon added furniture and carpet to its line and is still going strong on Forty-fourth Street near Clyde Park Avenue. (Brummel's Home Furnishings.)

Al and Bob's Sports has been supplying sports enthusiasts, particularly hunters and fishermen, for more than 50 years and is still located in the original store on Division Avenue. Merchandise is sold by knowledgeable staff in a personal atmosphere that chain stores can't duplicate. (Norma Lewis.)

Since 1951, the Leatherman Hardware store on Thirty-sixth Street has been serving the community in ways the so-called superstores never can. Where else can one grab the exact number of nails needed from a bin or buy a single link to fix a chain? At right, Robert Leatherman is inside his store in 1951; note the wagon on which he is sitting. In the image below, five generations of Leathermans and employees take time out for a photograph. (Leatherman Hardware.)

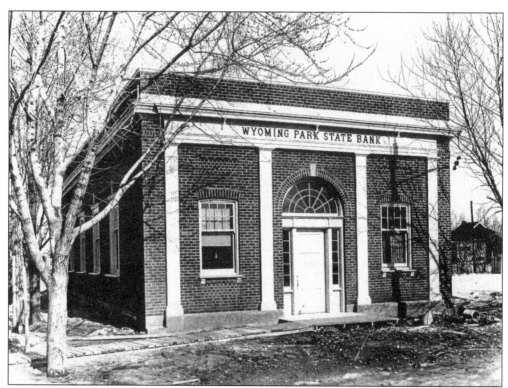

This photograph shows the comparatively modest building occupied by the Wyoming Park State Bank. Over the years, the bank expanded and maintained branch offices. (Wyoming Historical Commission.)

The Southwest Welding and Service Station was typical of the times when gas stations and service stations were one and the same. By the time Sherman and Angie Postma bought the business, an ice cream shop had been added. Many people, including of the authors of this book, have fond memories of stopping by for a chocolate cone. (Sherman and Angie Postma.)

Now known as Flowerland, Bob Tuinstra opened the original Fruit Basket in 1961. Participating in the ribbon-cutting ceremony are, from left to right, Doris Tuinstra, Lois Tuinstra, Bob Tuinstra, Sid Harkema, and Betty Harkema. The company is still headquartered at this Clyde Park Avenue and Twenty-eighth Street location and has additional stores in Kentwood and northwest Grand Rapids. (Flowerland.)

By the 1960s, people wanted manicured lawns, patios, and other outdoor living spaces. Fruit Basket Gardens filled the demand with plantings, outdoor furniture, and other decorative items, and free parking lured customers from Grand Rapids. (Flowerland.)

The long-awaited Rogers Plaza, Michigan's first indoor shopping mall, opened in August 1961 with Montgomery Ward and Kroger as its anchors. Below, among the people in this group photograph on hand for the opening ceremonies are Robert O. Bergman, Montgomery Ward local manager; Russell P. Bygel, Montgomery Ward vice president and regional manager; Karen Southway, Miss Michigan (third from left); C. L. Taylor, vice president of Grand Rapids Division Atlantic and Pacific food stores; Stanley Davis; Johannes C. Kolderman Jr., Wyoming mayor (second from right); and Joseph R. Sherry, vice president of Grand Rapids Division of Kroger Company. (Grand Rapids Public Library.)

By the end of 1961, Southland Plaza had opened on Michael Avenue across from Rogers Plaza and was anchored by Wurzburg's Department Store. The ribbon-cutting ceremony drew a large crowd. Note the sign on the building proclaiming that the store gave S and H Green Stamps, a major shopping incentive of the time. Herpolshimer's Department Store, popularly known as Herp's, replaced Wurzburg's in the mid-1970s. (Grand Rapids Public Library.)

Increased shopping opportunities attracted other leisure and entertainment facilities to the ever-growing Twenty-eighth Street. Restaurants proliferated, and the movies came too. Here children line up to buy snacks before watching the latest offering at Jack Loeks's movie theater. (Grand Rapids Public Library.)

The Log Cabin Bar-B-Q and cocktail lounge at 2401 South Division Avenue covered all its bases, offering fountain service, short orders, steak and chops, and dancing. It is still in business today, though the name has been shortened to simply the Log Cabin. (Grand Rapids Public Library.)

It seemed to be a major misjudgment when an unidentified motorist drove his vehicle into the lake at Lamar Park, drawing a large crowd of spectators. (Grand Rapids Public Library.)

Hattie Moss found some backyard shade to relax with her dog Sonia in the early 1940s while visiting her son on Beverly Street. (Anna Loomis DeWoolf.)

Three

SCHOOLS

Five school districts serve Wyoming: Wyoming, Kelloggsville, Godwin, and Godfrey-Lee, and the city's southwest panhandle is served by Grandville. Along with the public school system, Wyoming boasts private Christian schools, Catholic parochial schools, and Grace Bible College.

Wyoming's first school was founded on April 27, 1867. Augustine Godwin, supervisor of Wyoming Township and a Grand Valley pioneer, chaired the meeting that was held at the Godwin Hotel on Gull Prairie Road, now Division Avenue. Not surprisingly, the committee named the school Godwin. The first teacher, Charles Howard, was paid $1 a day, which no doubt included getting there early to start a fire in the stove and clean the building as needed.

School enrollment increased dramatically over the years. Until 1929, the Godwin Heights School was the largest of its kind in the nation. Other districts grew as well, and the city earned a reputation for providing good education coupled with excellent sports and extracurricular activities. Students who chose not to attend college left high school equipped to find work in the proliferating business and industrial venues throughout the township. One of the reasons factory owners decided to build in Wyoming was the capable and enthusiastic local work pool.

The Bowen School, a one-room building constructed by Bostwick Bowen, was completed in 1905. If it looks like a railroad depot, the reason is that the builder was ahead of his time and built the structure from recycled materials that had once been the Grand River Valley Railroad depot. In the image below, Bostwick rests on his Ford's bumper with, from left to right, sisters Cora and Jessie, with his wife, Ethel, to the far right. (Robert Kline.)

The eighth-grade graduating class of Newhall School poses for this c. 1915 photograph. From left to right they are (first row) Anna Van Dam, Mayme Syswerda, Mina Joyce, Jennie Vander Mark, Katherine Isenga; (second row) Walter Winfield, Elizabeth Baker, Thomas Kelder, and Jacob Van Dam. (Wyoming Historical Commission.)

This is believed to be a 1923 image of the Newhall School located at Thirty-sixth Street and Byron Center Avenue. (Wyoming Historical Commission.)

This is the first eighth-grade graduating class of the new Newhall Junior High School in 1958. The teachers are Mrs. Proud (far left, second row), Mr. Sullivan, Mr. Tower (second from the right, fourth row), and Mr. Mabry (to the right of Tower). (Wyoming Historical Commission.)

Class pictures, complete with teachers, bring back memories to all who appeared in such photographs. Here are two Newhall School pictures: the first grade is shown above, while the image below displays the seventh/eighth-grade class in 1961. (Wyoming Historical Commission.)

Godwin Has The Largest District School In The United States

History of Godwin Heights High School

New Godwin High School

Six years ago some people with foresight began to talk about the remarkable increase in the number of students at the little old brick school, among he oaks, at the corner of Division avenue and Allen Road. More people were able to see things and so after much argument it was voted to erect a new eight-room school building and thus Godwin Heights High School was born. School opened in September of 1923 and the first high school classes were organized. The Board of Education employed Charlie C. Saur as teacher of the 9th and 10th grades; at that time there were four other teachers in the grades. High School classes were first held in a Togan Stiles building, but were moved into the new building in January, 1924. There were 15 freshmen and 5 sophomores. Before the year was over there was not enough room in the new building to house the children and once more the taxpayers came together and voted for the north end addition which was ready in

January, 1925. In the fall of 1924 another teacher was added to the high school faculty and it was also at this time that Miss Gladys Irene Gaut came to have charge of the 8th grade. The number of students continued to increase and at the close of the 1924-25 school year the building was again too small. The south end addition was completed and occupied for the first time in December, 1927, and this was also too small to accommodate the number of students in 1928. In June, 1927 the first class of 5 members were graduated from Godwin —They were Alida Westers, Mildred Park, Esther VandenBerg, Josina VandenBerg and Marjorie Mohler. In 1928 twelve were graduated and now in 1929 seventeen more are added to the Alumni body of Godwin Heights School under the direction of Supt. Charlie C. Saur and Gladys I. Gaut. High School Principal has progressed rapidly and ranks very well with the other schools of Kent County in every way.

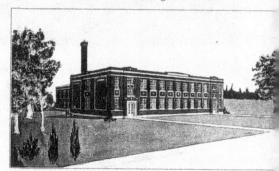

In 1929, the new Godwin Heights High School held the distinction of being the largest (kindergarten through grade 12) district school in the nation. (Ron Strauss.)

Frank Rackett was a Godwin Heights Board of Education member, natural history buff, and master taxidermist. He created a museum in the high school library to exhibit his collection. Here, in 1938, the Camp Fire Girls meet surrounded by many species of wildlife. (Ron Strauss.)

"We're all in our places, with bright shining faces," as the song implies, students came to school prepared to give teachers their full attention and learn everything they would need to know to make their way in the world as adults. (Wyoming Historical Commission.)

Godwin Heights High School students gather here for assembly in the school gym in the 1950s. The space also served as an auditorium. (Godwin School District.)

The Godwin Heights High School band and majorettes are seen here in full regalia. The photograph may be undated, but the girls' saddle shoes suggest it to be in the 1950s. Band teacher Anna Wald and her charges also marched in the Division Avenue Santa Claus Parade sponsored by merchant Earl Robson. (Godwin School District.)

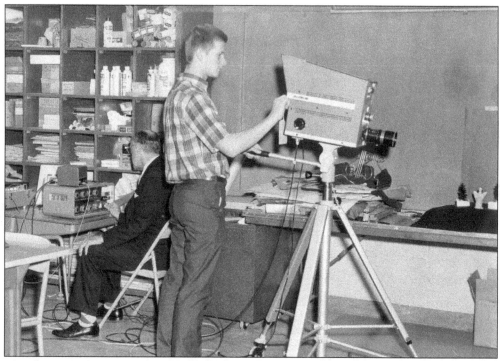

Closed-circuit television was used in Godwin in 1965 to benefit both students and parents. Student Jack Folkema learns to operate the electronic equipment with the help of Bill Obermeyer in the school's Media Center. (Godwin School District.)

Teachers in the 1960s had many audio-visual options to enhance their classroom lectures. This Godwin teacher chooses an opaque projector over the standard overhead preferred by some of the other instructors. (Godwin School District.)

These 1929 Lee School musicians are all dressed up and seem to be taking the whole situation quite seriously. (Grand Rapids Public Library.)

Also in the 1920s, a Lee drum major leads three strutting majorettes through the moves they will show in a parade. (Grand Rapids Public Library.)

School activities are greatly enhanced by parental involvement as shown by these four members of Wyoming Park High School's 1981 Varsity Club Boosters. Pictured from left to right are (first row) Nancy Bohrer and Sam Clinger; (second row) Don Wilson and Bob Burr. (Wyoming Park High School.)

Wyoming Park School kids received some unelected, but no doubt welcome, time off during the 1939 teacher's strike. (Grand Rapids Public Library.)

The 1981 Wyoming Park girls' varsity basketball team is suited up and ready for action. Pictured from left to right are (first row) Sharon Kellogg, Deb DeRoos, Jill Kole, Jennifer Griffin, and Brenda Schuitema; (second row) Stacey Snyder, Laura Erdmans, coach Rich Renzema, Kelly Mol, and Annette Barthel. (Wyoming Park High School.)

The 1981 Wyoming Park High School boys' swim team relaxes poolside. Pictured from left to right are (first row) Ed Griffen, Curt Grabill, Dan Goode, Brad Fleming, Bill Host, Brian DuBuis, Dave Harris, and Todd McNitt; (second row) manager Stacey Collins, Tom Land, coach Stan Pulaski, Paul Elderkin, Dave Pulaski, Tim Grabill, and Mark Clinger. (David Harris.)

Tri-Unity Christian School was founded by a group of parents seeking a Christ-centered, gospel-oriented education for their children. Above, elementary students enjoy being outside during recess. In the image below, the 1984 boys' basketball team benefited greatly from having Chris Kaman (no. 35, back row center) as a member. Kaman went on to play for Central Michigan University before going on to a professional career in the National Basketball Association (NBA). He currently plays for the Los Angeles Clippers. (Tri-Unity Christian School.)

Above is an aerial view of Grace Bible College's new complex in 1961. The institution moved to Wyoming from Milwaukee, Wisconsin, in 1960 and offered four-year degrees in various religious study disciplines under the leadership of Charles Baker in Milwaukee, Wisconsin, in 1932. The school celebrated its grand opening on October 31, 1961. (Grace Bible College.)

Students and faculty are setting up for a chapel service in the multipurpose chapel and cafeteria. (Grace Bible College.)

College president Charles F. Baker confers with students. The school enjoys a small student-teacher ratio that allows faculty to directly influence those under their tutelage. (Grace Bible College.)

Four

CHURCHES

The first Wyoming churches were established by the Dutch settlers, starting with the Grandville Avenue Christian Reformed Church in 1891. Because they were the largest immigrant group in the area, their church numbers reflect this. Of Wyoming's first 10 churches, 5 were of the Reformed or Christian Reformed denomination. They remain a majority, but a much smaller one.

Following soon were the Methodists, Brethren, Catholics, Baptists, and Lutherans. Religion played a larger role in the lives of the residents during the early days, so much so that few businesses opened on Sundays, and factory labor disputes sometimes centered around workers being required to work Sundays. While that was true in most places, it lasted in Wyoming well into the 1970s and early 1980s.

Today, in reflection of the changing times, some of the churches have primarily Hispanic or Asian congregations. Christ Lutheran Church on the corner of Eighty-fourth Street and Byron Center Avenue is also home to a second congregation called the Sudanese Christ Lutheran Church. The former Grandville Avenue Christian Reformed Church is now called the Roosevelt Park Community Christian Reformed and is proud of its success in providing multicultural services where the various populations worship together.

Gradually over the years, the city's churches have embraced the trend toward more informal contemporary services geared to appeal to the younger membership.

Grandville Avenue Christian Reformed Church organists pose with the new console. Seated is Albert Piersma, senior organist; standing from left to right are Albert Vanden Bosch, Mildred Bouman, and Joseph Van Beek. (Calvin College, Heritage Hall.)

The congregation joins together in song at the Roosevelt Park Community Christian Reformed Church, formerly the Grandville Avenue Christian Reformed Church. (*Grand Rapids Press.*)

The Holy Name Of Jesus Catholic Church has been a fixture on Godfrey Avenue since 1908. This congregation and choir photograph was taken in the 1940s, before the church moved to a new building in 1961. (Wyoming Historical Commission.)

The Wyoming Park Christian Reformed Church was established in 1919 on Twenty-eighth Street at Byron Center Avenue. The 1924 consistory was made up of, from left to right, (first row) Carl Storm, I. Siersema, Rev. E. B. Pekelder, John Groelsma Sr., and Clarence Hoeksema; (second row) Harm Huberts, Charles Plas, John Scuitema, and Gerrit Dyk. (Wyoming Park Christian Reformed Church.)

SUNDAY SCHOOL TEACHERS
First row: Mrs. John Pilon, Ruth Schilthuis, Mrs. Paul Schilthuis, Mrs. John Dykhouse.
Second row: Simon Van Dyken, Mrs. Jacob Haverkamp, Ann Reinsma, Marilyn Dykhouse, John Roelofs.
Third row: Cornelius Meekhof, John Van Solkema, Calvin Snoeyink, Clarence Van Dyken, Robert Beute.

Fifty years later, the 1969 Sunday school teachers pose for a special anniversary booklet honoring the church's history. (Wyoming Park Christian Reformed Church.)

Most churches have never been anything else. Some evolve from storefronts, and a few begin in private homes. Holy Trinity Episcopal, now located at 5333 Clyde Park Avenue, was a chicken coop on Burlingame Avenue when the church was established in 1957. (Holy Trinity Episcopal Church.)

Construction on the present Holy Trinity Episcopal began in 1961. Posing outside in 1962 are, from left to right, Fr. E. Ellis, Bob Nelson, C. Marsh, E. Drougel, G. Marrion, Orville Waterson, Bishop Bennislow, Dick Marrion, and unidentified. (Holy Trinity Episcopal Church.)

Wyoming Park Evangelical United Brethren Church prepares for its 1950 summer Bible school program. (Grand Rapids Public Library.)

Wyoming's First Assembly of God Church was organized in 1929 as the First Full Assembly of God. The entire congregation posed outside the Bellevue Avenue building in 1940. In 1977, the church built again, on a 28-acre lot on Forty-fourth Street, to meet the needs of its growing flock. The new building seats 1,400. (First Assembly of God Church.)

The Godwin Heights Choral Society was active in the 1930s. Members in place to perform are, from left to right, (first row) C. Boersma, J. Haveman, Mrs. C. Anthonsisse, Mrs. C. Baker, Mrs. J. Koster, G. Anthonisse, and R. Anthonisse; (second row) Mrs. J. Bult, Mrs. M. Reiffer, M. Reiffer, Mrs. J. Builema, J. Buikema, G. DeGroot, Mrs. J. Reiffer, Mrs. S. Reiffer, and Mrs. J. Dykema; (third row) G. Boersma, A. DeGroot, S. Reiffer Sr., H. Poll, director Henry Dice, J. Buikema, Rev. J. Bult, R. Brink, and M. Reiffer; (fourth row) N. Boersma, P. Reiffer, A. Reiffer, M. Reiffer, W. Poll, P. Albers, and J. Reiffer. (Calvin College, Heritage Hall.)

Gethsemane Lutheran Church has occupied the northeast corner of Clyde Park Avenue and Thirty-second Street since 1956. Above, the junior choir poses before singing during the 1981 anniversary year. Below, making up the 1981 church council are, from left to right, (first row) Sharon Sorensen, Mavis Davis, Lorraine LeFurge, and Sharlene Bowman; (second row) Joyce Koppenhofer, Clay Royce, Pete Parker, and Pastor Kenneth Johnson; (third row) Jim Vandergom, Bud Lees, Al Metzner, and Bob Lymburner. (Gethsamane Lutheran Church.)

Five

EVERYDAY LIFE IN WYOMING

There has never been a shortage of things to do in Wyoming, but the earliest settlers worked long days, and when they did have some free time it was often filled with church picnics or other social events. Buck Creek provided a picnic spot, and just visiting with neighbors was considered a treat. In the 1930s, when no one had money for entertainment, Earl Robson hung a sheet on a basement wall of his Division department store and showed movies for an appreciative local crowd.

When residents did have the opportunity to spend some entertainment dollars, Wyoming has provided several venues. Bigelow Field hosted local teams and major-league exhibition games. Other events held there included major entertainers, like Bob Hope, who did a show in 1946.

Lamar Park had a sandy beach for swimmers along with other outdoor recreation opportunities. From 1963 to the mid-1980s, it was the site of an annual rodeo that attracted stars such as Ken Curtis, who played Festus Haggens, Marshal Matt Dillon's sidekick on *Gunsmoke*. The last two years consisted of bull riding only.

One of the area's earliest flea markets still operates on summer weekends at what was once the drive-in movie theater on Twenty-eighth Street between Burlingame and Michael Avenues.

The Grand Rapids Tackers, a Midwest Professional Basketball League team, played home games at Godwin High School Fieldhouse.

Over the years, Wyoming has offered ever-increasing social and entertainment options. And with the addition of Rogers Department Store and the Wyoming Village Mall, Twenty-eighth Street became a shopping mecca that drew people from Grand Rapids and beyond.

William and Rose Strauss had two reasons to be proud: the birth of their first child Roger and a shiny black Ford. In the image below, William is placing the baby on the hood to better display both. He sold his drums to raise money for the car. (Ron Strauss.)

A warm day and a cozy quilt are all it takes to keep Caroline Loomis happy while the adults go on with their chores. Caroline is the daughter of Alice and Benjamin Loomis. (Anna Loomis DeWoolf.)

Always ready for a little girl talk, Alice Loomis and her sister-in-law Margaret Loomis (sitting on the stump), who is visiting from Kalamazoo, take a time out to chat. (Anna Loomis DeWoolf.)

It looked like a fashion show when these ladies donned their stylish winter coats and posed in front of Olide Visser's (third from left) house in 1923. (Wyoming Historical Commission.)

When Peter Stalsonburg wasn't using horse-drawn machinery to dig basements for new houses in the burgeoning township, he enjoyed hitching the horses to his buggy and taking his grandchildren for rides. (Wyoming Historical Commission.)

It was 1929 when these three cousins stepped outside for a group photograph. Edwin Cassidy puts an arm around flappers Irene Chapman (left) and Ernestine Chapman. The Chapman family lived just off Lee Street in Wyoming Park from 1924 through 1933. (Kate Chapman.)

Sears was the go-to retailer in the early decades of the 20th century. The mail-order giant sold everything, from clothing to tools and household goods—even prefabricated houses. So it wasn't much of a leap to order a Sears motorbike. (Wyoming Historical Commission.)

With George Visser playing violin
while accompanied by his wife,
Olide, on the pump organ, the couple
made beautiful music together. They
emigrated from the Netherlands and
established a large, close-knit family in
their new country. The organ, along
with the silver tea service shown in the
image below, indicates they probably
had some money when they came
and further flourished in America.
(Wyoming Historical Commission.)

As people began having a little more spare time, they looked for satisfying ways to fill it. Sunday painters proliferated. This artist on the right has chosen his house as his subject. The image below indicates he was pleased enough with his effort to have a gathering to show it. (Wyoming Historical Commission.)

Weddings have come in all styles. The formal attire of George and Caroline (Moser) Franklin in this *c.* 1910 photograph indicates they tied the knot in a church or other venue that would accommodate guests. After the wedding, the couple lived in the Godfrey area. (Joanna Franklin Overmeyer.)

Mr. and Mrs. Olson chose a simpler route to marital bliss and were married on November 17, 1946, in the Wyoming Township office of the justice of the peace. (Grand Rapids Public Library.)

George Rose, owner of the 84-year Burton Street icon the Rose Shoe, catches a ride on the running board of the family vehicle. For many years, the Roses lived just down the road from the store. (Ron Strauss.)

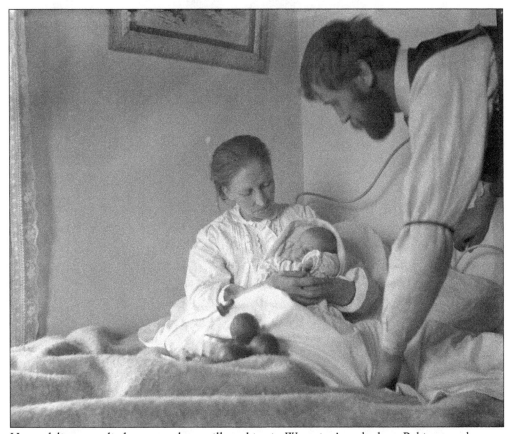

Home delivery applied to more than milk and ice in Wyoming's early days. Babies were born at home, often without the assistance of a doctor. It is unclear whether the man leaning over the mother and child is a doctor or the father. (Wyoming Historical Commission.)

Trains played an important role in Wyoming's early history. The interurban, which made stops in the city during its runs to Kalamazoo and Holland, provided easy transportation on a daily basis. The Fisher Station was on the Kalamazoo route. (Grand Rapids Public Library.)

Grand Rapids needed a new airport, and these supporters thought a model would help sell the idea. In 1926, the Kent County Airport opened on the portion of Madison Avenue that is now called Roger B. Chaffee Drive in memory of the astronaut who perished in a launch-pad explosion with Edward White and Virgil (Gus) Grissom. (Grand Rapids Public Library.)

Above, this car knocker worked at
the Chesapeake and Ohio rail yard in
Wyoming and is shown making his
inspections in February 1950. The image
to the right depicts the greenhouses
at the C&O yard in September of
1951. (Grand Rapids Public Library.)

The airport welcomed many celebrities over the years. Arguably one of the most popular, Lassie arrives for a Grand Rapids appearance. (Grand Rapids Public Library.)

Along with commercial flights, single-engine private planes, like the Aercoupe shown here, kept the airport busy. When the airport outgrew its Wyoming space in 1963, a new facility was built east of Wyoming and named the Gerald R. Ford International Airport in honor of the late president. (Grand Rapids Public Library.)

Almar Rice tunes his radio, perhaps to listen to *Fibber McGee and Molly*, while his son August snaps this photograph with a Brownie camera in 1939. (Wyoming Historical Commission.)

Grace and Elvin Feenstra pose with Jack the cat in their cozy living room on Avon Street in Wyoming Park around 1940. (Joanna and James Boone.)

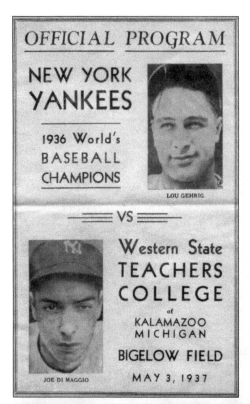

The New York Yankees played Western State Normal at Bigelow Field on May 3, 1937. They were the reigning champions, having won the 1936 World Series. The official program featured Yankee team members Lou Gehrig and Joe Dimaggio. (Robert Kline.)

Midget auto races were big events: fun to work on, fun to race, and were opportunities for fathers and sons to bond at the track. This confident-looking young man raced at Bigelow Field in August 1950. (Wyoming Public Library.)

Mickey Cochrane, manager and coach of the Great Lakes Naval Training Station baseball team in north Chicago, Illinois, appeared at Bigelow Field in 1943. He is shown here returning a salute from eight-year-old Arthur J. Newhouse of Grand Rapids. The boy had presented Cochrane with a Detroit Tigers scrapbook covering the 1934 and 1935 seasons when Cochrane played for the team. (Grand Rapids Public Library.)

The four members of the dolly club dressed themselves and their dolls as elegantly as possible for events that included tea parties. They obtained some of their finery by raiding their mothers' closets for shoes and other necessities. The girls all lived in the same Godwin Heights neighborhood. From left to right they are Eloise Sparks, Phyllis Hudson, Dorothy Thomas, and Marilyn Hudson. (Ron Strauss.)

The annual rodeo held at Lamar Park drew large crowds and big-name stars for more than 20 years. Here a cowboy demonstrates his moves to city folks. (Wyoming Historical Commission.)

In August 1942, long before female firefighters were a familiar presence in fire stations across the country, these women were instructed on how the equipment works and given the chance to demonstrate their new skills. This might have been the first time a dress was seen peeking out from under a rubber fireman's coat. (Grand Rapids Public Library.)

Grappling with a heavy hose while climbing a ladder probably wasn't as easy as these women made it look. (Grand Rapids Public Library.)

Wyoming Township firemen were justifiably proud of their shiny trucks and equipment in 1941. (Wyoming Historical Commission.)

In 1939, some photographers found it lucrative to travel through residential neighborhoods, costumes and pony in tow, to capture the likenesses of young cowboy wannabes. Here, with his hat slightly askew, is two-year-old Jack Schultz. (Wyoming Historical Commission.)

World War II captured the imaginations of children in 1943, and these boys were no exception. Maurice "Pug" Blish (leaning in front) is digging a foxhole with, from left to right, Terry O'Rourke, Gordon Frost, and Jack Schultz to be ready in the event of an enemy attack. The house is at 1119 Wheeler Street. (Wyoming Historical Commission.)

Nothing exemplifies summer like swaying on a shaded porch swing. And while they were swinging, Jack Schultz (left), Terry O'Rourke (center), and Maurice "Pug" Blish weren't getting into mischief. (Wyoming Historical Commission.)

Victory gardens did more than put food on the table in the ration-stamp World War II days. Tending them provided family companionship in the summer sun. This Wyoming garden was photographed in 1943. (Grand Rapids Public Library.)

Women accepted responsibility for raising funds to support the local school districts, which involved everything from organizing bake sales, "second-best" sales, and even knocking on doors, as shown here when Wyoming Park needed a new athletic field in 1950. (Grand Rapids Public Library.)

Lamar Park often hosted games for the member teams of the city's industrial leagues. Shown here are players from Kelvinator, Saint Alphonsus, Brann's, and South Wyoming Merchants. (Grand Rapids Public Library.)

Before the days when most women began working outside the home, they filled some of their daytime hours with community and club work, as well as pursuing hobbies. This collector readies her dolls for a Wyoming Park craft and hobby show in January 1945. (Grand Rapids Public Library.)

Needlework was another popular pastime, and it was always fun to share one's interests with others. Another exhibitor at the craft and hobby show poses with her crocheted doilies. It can only be speculated at the hours that went into this creation. (Grand Rapids Public Library.)

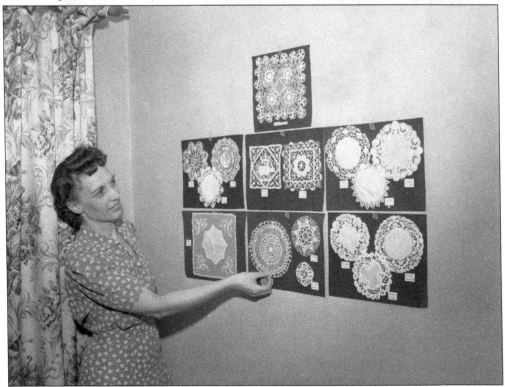

The Godfrey Lee School District must have been proud of the large number of girls turning out for Girl Scouts. Here they take advantage of a nice day to sit on the school lawn for a group photograph. (Wyoming Historical Commission.)

Boys are naturally drawn to scouting, and those in Kelloggsville were no exception. The costumed Boy Scout Cubs are making a joyful noise in their den mother's living room in 1950. (Grand Rapids Public Library.)

Scouting was an important part of a
boy's life in Godwin Heights in the
1960s and 1970s. An especially enjoyable
time was a weekend spent at this
Kelloggsville log cabin. (Ron Strauss.)

The children of Clarence and Mary Koetje
pose here in 1951. From front to back
are Glenn, Russell, Gerald, and Wilma.
(Wyoming Historical Commission.)

Clarence Koetje makes hay while the sun shines on the family farm. His wife, Mary, takes time out from her endless chores for a brief rest in the shade and a smile to preserve the moment for history. Both photographs were taken in mid- to late 1949. (Wyoming Historical Commission.)

A grim reminder of the dangers faced by those in law enforcement occurred when officer Bill Catlin counted the bullet holes in the hood of his patrol car. (Wyoming Police Department.)

Of course police work has its gratifying moments too. Wyoming Township officers Jerry Lanninga (left) and Don Stratton delivered this baby in October 1945. (Wyoming Police Department.)

By the 1960s, every city's police department had an Officer Friendly, a school-visiting officer whose job was to instill in each child that officers are their friends. The popular Wyoming version was officer Harold Ergang, a ventriloquist, who shared the stage with his uniformed alter ego, Danny Dugan. (Wyoming Police Department.)

Little League football teaches young athletes the value of teamwork and sportsmanship. Lamar Park was the home field for the 1969 champion Wildcats pictured here. (Ron Strauss.)

This *c.* 1950s postcard shows the inviting beach at Lamar Park, which remained open until 2007. Over the years, the park was home to many events, including an annual rodeo, Fourth of July fireworks displays, concerts, and more. (Norma Lewis.)

The Lamar Park lake was put to good use in winter as well as summer. Neighborhood kids and adults enjoyed ice-skating throughout Michigan's long winters. (Ron Strauss.)

Casting a line into the water on a warm summer day was just one of the pleasurable activities for which Wyoming's parks were created. (Wyoming Parks and Recreation Department.)

Local Wyoming sharpshooter Jill Ann Brunette practices her sport at the Grand Rapids Rifle and Pistol Club in 1958. (Grand Rapids Public Library.)

Residents of Thirty-fourth Street, east of Division Avenue, put up elaborate Christmas displays during the mid-1900s. This life-size nativity scene is an example of the decorations that sometimes stopped traffic when the crowds came to look. (Robert Kline.)

Department store and mall Santas draw children in droves. Before Rogers Plaza opened, Wyoming's choice Santa spot was the front window of the Robson Department Store. Robson's had several Santas, but Owen Barney, shown here, was the favorite. For many years, Earl Robson also sponsored a Santa Claus Parade down Division Avenue to further enhance his customers' holiday spirit. The parade was followed by gifts of candy and peanuts to the children. (Wyoming Historical Commission.)

Music or dance lessons were mandatory in some families, and Earl Robson's daughters Bonnie (left) and Sandra (right) opened a music school where they taught youngsters to play the accordion. Both were accomplished musicians, as was their mother, Ann, and the three Robsons often played for weddings and other social events. (Wyoming Historical Commission.)

In 1969, Ron Strauss was selected to represent Michigan at the Presidential Youth Conference. It was during Richard Nixon's presidency, so that honor made him a guest at the Republican Convention. He is pictured here with Gerald R. Ford (left), Arnold Palmer (second from left), and Detroit Red Wing legend Gordie Howe (right). (Ron Strauss.)

The whole country mourned when Roger B. Chaffee, along with Virgil "Gus" Grissom and Edward White, died in a launchpad explosion. Wyoming especially felt the loss. Chaffee never lived here, but his parents moved to the city from Grand Rapids when he was in training. They were still residents at the time of his death. The Roger B. Chaffee Industrial Park and street bear his name, as does the local American Legion post. Grand Rapids boasts the Roger B. Chaffee Planetarium. At right, the astronaut and his parents get a grand tour of Cape Canaveral. Below, it is business as usual as Chaffee (far left) is interviewed in front of a command module. (Grand Rapids Public Museum.)

The Wyoming Library still boasts the highest attendance in the Kent District Library. Through the years, it has maintained a kid-friendly atmosphere, as shown in this c. 1955 image—a scene duplicated many times over. Styles have changed but not the attention to detail shown by the library's dedicated staff. (Grand Rapids Public Library.)

Chris Kaman, a center for the NBA's Los Angeles Clippers, graduated from Tri-Unity Christian High School in Wyoming. He went on to Central Michigan University, where he played three seasons before turning professional after being drafted by the Clippers in 2003. He became a dual citizenship holder (United States and Germany) so that he could play basketball with the German team in the 2008 Beijing Olympics. In the qualifying tournament, he achieved a "double-double" with 10 points and 10 rebounds. (National Basketball Association.)

Six

LOOKING AHEAD

Rogers Plaza is no longer the retail draw it once was but offers the convenience of a Secretary of State office, Big Boy, Old Country Buffet, and a post office. The anchors are a Family Fare supermarket and Office Max, so the retail shops do get traffic, though there are always vacancies. The area was further hurt when the upscale Rogers Department Store closed. Robert Israels brought new life to the area in 2008, when he moved his Klingman fine furnishings store into the space.

The Grand Rapids area has become the forefront of health care in southwest Michigan, and Wyoming facilities, such as the new Metro Hospital and other urgent care and outpatient services, enhance the growing medical corridor.

The city boasts 21 parks, not including the Kent Trails walking and bike path that goes through the city. Wyoming has always had ample parks for its residents to enjoy. The newest, a dog park, is located on Nagle Avenue. Access to the outdoors is never far away for those pursuing year-round recreational opportunities.

In August 2009, Wyoming celebrated its first 50 years as an incorporated city. Now looking toward the next 50, city officials are working hard to make sure it lives up to its reputation as a city of vision and progress.

Nothing demonstrates the city's growing diversity more than its churches. As each new population gains sufficient numbers, it establishes a house of worship. A Sudanese congregation meets at the Christ Lutheran Church located on the corner of Byron Center Avenue and Forty-fourth Street. In the photograph above, some of the members pose outside their church, while the pastor, Matthew Rial, preaches in the image below. (Sudanese Christ Lutheran Church.)

An increasing number of area churches are conducting services in Spanish. Wyoming's Latin American population is made up of immigrants from Mexico, Cuba, the Dominican Republic, San Salvador, Guatemala, and other Spanish-speaking countries. The Elim Reformed Church shown here is located just north of Twenty-eighth Street. (Norma Lewis.)

In 1992, the Hahn-In Korean congregation acquired the former Wyoming Park Christian Reformed Church building on Twenty-eighth Street at Byron Center Avenue, where it serves one of Wyoming's growing Asian populations. (Norma Lewis.)

Wyoming's future is important, but so is its past, and the Wyoming Historical Commission makes sure it isn't forgotten. Here Bill Branz, coauthor of *Wilderness to Wyoming*, shows some of the commission's treasures. The collection is housed in the Wyoming Public Library. (Jay de Vries.)

The annual Metro Cruise brings automobile enthusiasts from around southwest Michigan each year to see the displays and join the festivities that stretch along Twenty-eighth Street through Wyoming and Kentwood. (Kentwood Chamber of Commerce.)

Still a Wyoming fixture, Marge's Donut Den made the news in early 2010 when the bakery provided guitar-shaped donuts and a decorated cake for country music star Brad Paisley and his entourage when they performed at De Vos Hall in Grand Rapids. Shane (right) and Shelby Ayers enjoy the everyday fare served here: scrumptious donuts, preferably with hot chocolate. (Norma Lewis.)

Rogers Plaza isn't the shopping mecca it once was, but with a Family Fare supermarket, Office Max, a Secretary of State office, Big Boy, Old Country Buffet, and other shops, it still draws traffic into the area. Hattie (left) and Bella Berry, who live on Delwood Avenue in the Godfrey Lee neighborhood, enjoy a shopping break. (Norma Lewis.)

Long vacant, the old Reynolds Metals plant is now partially occupied by Land and Company, the family business of Secretary of State Terry Lynn Land. (Norma Lewis.)

When Robert Israels relocated his Klingman's Furniture Store in the old Rogers Department Store building on Twenty-eighth Street, it gave new life to the area and was a positive sign for the city's future. A stalwart in the local retail furniture industry, Israels operated another store in the Grand Rapids area, Israels Designs for Living. Both stores closed in the early fall of 2010. (Norma Lewis.)

Leading Wyoming into the future are city manager Curtis Holt, shown at left, and the city council. City council members shown above are, from left to right, William Ver Hulst, Richard Pastoor, city attorney Jack Sluiter, Curtis Holt, Mayor Jack Pohl, city clerk Heidi Isakson, Sam Bolt, and Dan Burrill. Council members Joanne Voorhees and Kent Underwood were absent. (City of Wyoming.)

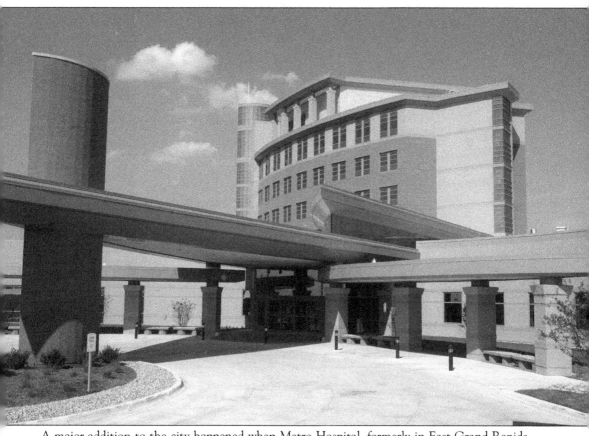

A major addition to the city happened when Metro Hospital, formerly in East Grand Rapids, constructed its new campus here. The facility is located on Byron Center Avenue and M-6. St. Mary's Hospital opened a new urgent care and outpatient facility on the other side of M-6 in Byron Center. (Metro Hospital.)

Visit us at
arcadiapublishing.com

Printed in the USA
CPSIA information can be obtained
at www.ICGtesting.com
LVHW070743121223
766160LV00008B/95